Candy Cane Lane's Story

Sister Mary Faith

Robert J. Marek.
EDITOR

Candy Cane Lane's Story

iUniverse books may be ordered through booksellers or by contacting:

iUniverse
1663 Liberty Drive
Bloomington, IN 47403
www.iuniverse.com
1-800-Authors (1-800-288-4677)

ISBN: 978-1-5320-8939-8 (sc)
ISBN: 978-1-5320-8940-4 (hc)
ISBN: 978-1-5320-8941-1 (e)

Library of Congress Control Number: 2019919616

Print information available on the last page.

iUniverse rev. date: 12/04/2019

Candy Cane Lane's Story

DEDICATION PAGE

This book is dedicated to all the children of the world. Jesus loves all the little children, all the little children of the world. Red & yellow, black & white, they are precious in His sight.

- C. Herbert Woolston

Mrs. Cane found out she was going to be a mommy. She shared this wonderful news with her husband.

When Mr. Cane found out he was going to be a daddy, he was very happy and excited.

Mr. and Mrs. Cane wanted their baby to feel loved from the very beginning, so Mrs. Cane held her baby close to her heart.

Mrs. Cane started craving more and more candy. Her doctor said that it was okay to eat a little more candy. He laughed and said, "You are going to have a sweet little girl. Why not name her Candy?"

Mrs. Cane told her husband about the doctor's idea. Mr. Cane liked the name. Her name would be Candy Cane.

One evening in December, Mrs. Cane went to the hospital to have her little baby girl. Mrs. Cane looked at her daughter for the very first time.

Candy was a very beautiful baby. People at the hospital thought she was a very sweet baby too!

SKILL
ATTITUDE
EDUCATION
SELF
DEVELOPMENT
RELATIONSHIP
PASSION
EXPERIENCE

Candy Cane grew up to be just as sweet as a woman. She loved people and used many ideas to help them.

Everyone wanted to do something in her honor. Someone suggested naming a street after her. Now people celebrate her birth in December. That is how Candy Cane Lane came to be!

Merry Christmas!

Photographic Credits

Cover page: iStock 1126840570; credit: ratmaner

Page 1: iStock 637997768; credit: kupicoo

Page 2: iStock 584772264; credit: kupicoo

Page 3: iStock 640220198; credit: PeopleImages

Page 4: iStock 840904822; credit: Wavebreakmedia

Page 5: iStock 669459204; credit: TTP6

Page 6: iStock 178541567; credit: Wavebreakmedia

Page 7: iStock 867921622; credit: aywan88

Page 8: iStock 450161131; credit: SirlkulT

Page 9: iStock 184936717; credit: constantgardener

Printed in the United States
By Bookmasters